CHRISTIANS
GRIEVE
TOO

CHRISTIANS GRIEVE TOO

Donald Howard

THE BANNER OF TRUTH TRUST

THE BANNER OF TRUTH TRUST
3 Murrayfield Road, Edinburgh EH12 6EL
P.O. Box 621, Carlisle, Pennsylvania, 17013, U.S.A.

*

© aio PUBLISHING — SYDNEY 1979

FIRST PUBLISHED BY aio PUBLISHING
St. Andrew's House, Sydney Square, NSW 2000
1979

FIRST BANNER OF TRUTH EDITION 1980
Reprinted 1986
Reprinted 1993
Reprinted 1998

ISBN 0 85151 315 8

In appreciation of those who have learned to "bear one another's burdens and so fulfil the law of Christ." (Galatians 6:2)

CONTENTS

Preface

When C. S. Lewis wrote of his wife's death, his opening words were, "No one ever told me. . ."

At the age of 40, my wife contracted breast cancer. The happy and active mother of four teenage children, her life soon resumed with a favourable prognosis after successful surgery.

Over a year later she suffered a rapid loss in weight. The organism was in the bone and further surgery was necessary. Her life expectancy was six to eighteen months, but she enjoyed reasonable health for another four years. The end came nearly two years ago when she was aged 46.

Encouraged by family and friends, and fortified through faith in Christ, we were prepared for death.

But I was ill-prepared for grief, for "No one ever told me. . ."

DONALD HOWARD
Sydney, Australia
August 1979.

The Reality of Grief

"Yea, though I walk through the valley of the shadow of death,
I will fear no evil; for thou art with me; thy rod and staff
shall comfort me."
(Psalm 23)

We often talk of grief, some of us have experienced it, but do we know how to cope with it? Are we able to help others who grieve? Do we know what to say, how to act? Above all, does the Christian faith enable us to know the comfort which our Lord promises in the verse above?

The Bible regards grief as a very real thing. The word it uses signifies sorrow, pain, or a wound. It applies mainly to sorrow of soul, such as that of the disciples at the imminent death of Jesus.

"Grief", says Jay Adams, "may be called a life-shaking sorrow over loss. Grief tears life to shreds; it shakes one from top to bottom. It pulls a person loose; he comes apart at the seams. Grief is truly nothing less than a life-shattering loss."

Those who grieve over death are called *"bereaved"*. The word "reave" means to commit ravages, to forcibly deprive or take by force. A "bereaved" person is literally one who is broken up in what is an intensely personal experience.

Bereavement describes the whole reaction to loss; it includes the emotional response and our adjustment to that loss. One's thought, feeling and behaviour are so drastically affected that the condition may be viewed as an illness.

9

That is why, in the first year of bereavement, widows and widowers have a death rate ten times as great as that of a similar segment of the population which has not been bereaved.

Bereavement has been associated with psychiatric and physiological illness. Tuberculosis, ulcerative colitis, obesity, rheumatoid arthritis, heart failure and even cancer have been associated with bereavement. Sometimes the bereaved person will take on the symptoms of the deceased's illness.

Grief is not confined to the death of a loved one. A move from the "old family home", loss of possessions, money, job, health; the death of a pet, the marriage of a member of the family, can be just as devastating as death. In divorce, the grief may be even worse because there is not the finality of death.

Children probably experience grief far more than we realise. The young are prone to attacks of grief which older people may not experience in similar situations. The glib advice given when a romance is broken, that "there are plenty more fish in the sea", reveals an ignorance that real grief may be produced by such an upset.

In death, grief is a reality not only for the survivors, but for the person dying. The survivors lose one person, but the dying one loses every earthly relationship.

It is for the "survivors" that this is written.

Grief caused by death is more than a crisis; it is a process. Some see as many as ten "stages" involved, with the process varying according to the person and the situation. The acute phase may last three months; where it extends beyond that, highly skilled attention may be necessary.

Well over 12 months after my bereavement, I visited the wife of a friend dying in similar circumstances. It was impossible to control my emotions. For several days afterwards I needed the ministry of Christian friends during a period of emotional and physical exhaustion.

I had talked about grief and supposedly faced the facts. I had mourned and wept, but there were still unknown depths of unexpressed grief. Self-diagnosis is somewhat unreliable, but I believe that my emotional state is only now returning to what it was four or five years ago.

By contrast, a sudden death, particularly that of a young child, will produce vastly different reactions. "Natural" deaths due to age and infirmity will generally be different again.

Fortunately, the Christian enjoys benefits in contrast to the society about him which is "without hope and without God in the world".[1] His hope is more than a wish or a desire; it is living and sure: a confident assurance based upon the person and work of the Lord Jesus Christ.

About 700 years before our Lord was born, Isaiah the prophet described Jesus as a "man of sorrows and acquainted with grief".[2] His grief was expressed for others, as when He wept at the grave of His friend Lazarus and mourned over the city of Jerusalem.[3] He also knew what it was to grieve for Himself. A few hours before His own betrayal and death, His humanity endured such suffering in Gethsemane that "His sweat was like drops of blood falling to the ground."[4]

Great though His grief was, He went to the cross, that through the perfect sacrifice of Himself He might secure the salvation of His people from their sins.[5] The person who acknowledges Jesus Christ as absolute king of his life receives

1. Ephesians 2:12   2. Isaiah 53:3
3. John 11:25f.; Matthew 23:27f   4. Luke 22:44
5. cf. Hebrews 5:9, 9:26; Matthew 1:21

forgiveness of sins and enjoys a personal relationship with Jesus made real by the Holy Spirit.[6] This bond is particularly meaningful in grief, because Jesus shared our earthly experiences, including suffering and death. Hence He is able to help us and sympathise with us.[7]

This is more than wishful thinking. The Christian's confidence is based upon a fact of history — Jesus rose to life from the dead! He was crucified and raised on our behalf,[8] so that we trust not a dead Saviour but a risen Lord.[9] In fact, without the resurrection, our faith would be worthless.[10] The resurrection shows that God accepted Christ's sacrifice on the cross and it vindicates His claims to Lordship.

There is also a future aspect which encourages us. Peter told his readers that, on the basis of the resurrection, we should one day have an inheritance in heaven.[11] This will not be an "airy fairy" existence, because our bodies are to be raised and we shall continue to share in fellowship with Christ and with our loved ones who die believing in Him.[12]

What a unique privilege it is to be a Christian! Jesus not only experienced and overcame grief, but death itself. We do not face these experiences alone, but in the strength which He provides.

Nevertheless, we do grieve, and the knowledge of what to expect when grief comes will better enable us to cope with it.

6. Acts 16:30f.; Acts 10:43   7. Hebrews 2:18, 4:15
8. Romans 4:25   9. Romans 14:9   10. 1 Corinthians 15:19
11. 1 Peter 1:3f   12. 1 Corinthians 15; Ephesians 2:6f

The Experience of Grief

"Mary stood outside the tomb crying."
(John 20:11)

Most doctors regard shock as the initial symptom of grief. A healthy emotional outlet, shock should not cause alarm; neither should it be prolonged. The person affected by shock finds it impossible to grasp fully what has happened. There may be general disorganization and an inability to face facts, a phase which may last for hours, days, or even weeks.

Despite an outburst of emotion, death is not accepted. The bereaved may act as though nothing had happened. The "radiance" of some at a funeral may be symptomatic of shock rather than of Christian faith.

Those in shock may experience numbness, the feeling of being stunned, hysteria, a near or an actual paralysis and bewilderment. In other words, there are *physical symptoms*.

Physical distress may come in waves of bodily discomfort deep down inside. There may be a tight feeling in the throat, a feeling of being suffocated, deep sighing (without the sufferer realizing it). He may go around saying "Oh my" or something like that.

Some suffer a drained emotional state, emptiness of feeling, a sense of unreality or quite deep depression. There is often the thought that "it can't really be true".

Loss of spirit, zest, joy, initiative and motivation can be expected, along with laziness. Planning seems useless, if not

13

impossible. What is done tends to be done mechanically. In personal dealings, there may be stiffness and formality, even with close friends.

Intense pining and loneliness may begin to show themselves, even though the loss is not yet fully realized. Mental anguish may be experienced. The bereaved wife may think that she sees her husband or hears his voice or that he is in bed beside her. This illusion is a normal response.

Some have a yearning to find the lost person again. They will visit places of happy memory. Over the next few weeks, the bereaved may be preoccupied with memories of the dead person.

In my own case, I cannot recall any shock — rather a feeling of relief, coupled with the emotional release of weeping. This was probably because much grief had been experienced beforehand. Over the next few weeks particularly, tears were shed on several occasions.

At times there was a reserve towards others, often as a defence against well-meaning people who were clumsy in their approach.

On looking back, I realize how little most of us really know about the whole process, both in personal grief and in helping those in need.

Complications in Grief

"If we confess our sins, He is faithful and righteous to forgive us our sins and to cleanse us from all unrighteousness."
(1 John 1:9)

In coping with grief, other emotions such as guilt, anger and fear may be involved. Once we are aware of this, we are better able to deal with our own grief or to support others.

Guilt is associated with grief far more than most people are aware. It can cause serious complications, particularly where death is sudden.

The driver of a car involved in an accident will reproach himself about his speed, his direction or time of travel; the mother of a child who suffers an accident in the home will regret inattention on her part — real or supposed.

Sometimes the "guilt" may be irrational or neurotic. A friend told me that one night before his wife died, the family had viewed slides from their holidays over the years. "If only I had thought of that!" was my reaction.

Where it is possible to grieve together before death, many possible factors which might cause later guilt can be eliminated. The last few weeks that my wife and I spent with one another were some of the closest in over 26 years together. We laughed, we cried, we recalled moments of intimacy and joy, the occasions when we had experienced differences and misunderstanding.

My main regret is that we did not discuss the future more, but there was always the hope that, her life having been prolonged longer than was expected, there might still be a reprieve. (Ironically, it was through her reading on death and grief that she was able to encourage me).

Where sudden death has ruptured a relationship, sin unconfessed and unforgiven can cause serious complications. This should prompt us to seek to live peaceably with others, to pray about our everyday contacts and to know the love of Christ controlling us in our dealings with family, friends and acquaintances. Paul's advice is worth following, "Do not let the sun go down while you are still angry."[13]

I once ministered to a widow who claimed (perhaps with justification) that she had been cheated over 30 years before when a family business was sold. She always told me of the alleged dishonesty of her brother-in-law, who had later died. Each time the tale concluded with the same words: "I think I've forgiven him, haven't I, Mr. Howard?"

Had she?

Often the "guilty" party will mention the matter spontaneously soon after the death has occurred. Even if imaginary and without foundation, the matter is real to the sufferer and must be discussed. One must never say, "There's nothing to be guilty about."

Perhaps skilled counsel may be needed at a later date when the initial emotional reaction has subsided. The counsellor may then ask, "Do you remember telling me. . . ?" Or there may be wisdom in words such as, "Often one feels guilty at a time like this, wondering whether one might have done more, or wishing that one had not had that last argument — it could help if we could talk about any feelings like this that you might have."

Where guilt does appear to be rational, there must be

13. Ephesians 4:26

compassionate teaching on repentance. This may appear cruel or harsh, but sorrow alone does not bring relief when sin needs to be confessed. Esau "was rejected. He could bring about no change of mind, though he sought the blessing with tears."[14] There is one solution to give the guilty conscience peace: "the blood of Jesus . . . purifies us from all sin."[15]

Protest and anger are often evident in the bereaved. Criticism may be directed againt God ("if there is one"). Sometimes it is directed against the dead person — "He should have driven more carefully" — "I told her to see the doctor" — "He left me just when I needed him most", and so on.

Doctors, hospital staff or ministers are often targets for hostility. The minister has usually "neglected visiting". The doctor either made "a faulty diagnosis" or "performed an unnecessary operation". Of course, where there are firm grounds for such charges, the hostility is understandable, but it must nevertheless be brought to the Lord for removal.

Like guilt, anger must be exposed, discussed and dealt with.

Another complicating factor in bereavement is fear.

My wife expressed fear — whether the pain might become unbearable or whether her faith might fail before the end. Thankfully, both fears were groundless.

On the other hand, I feared the future without the one whose life had been shared with mine. Such fear is very real. The words with which C. S. Lewis began were, "No one ever told me that grief felt so like fear. I am not afraid, but the sensation is like being afraid. The same fluttering in the stomach, the same restlessness, the yawning. I keep on swallowing."

The Christian may have to admit the reality of this fear, but does he also have the understanding of God's providence that enables him to overcome it? It is surprising how people

14. Hebrews 12:17   15. 1 John 1:7

who read their Bibles fail to appreciate that God's providential care extends over every circumstance in life and that "perfect love drives out fear."[16]

"What are God's works of providence?" asks the Shorter Catechism. The reply rings back, ". . .His most holy, wise, and powerful preserving and governing all His creatures and all their actions." This is an endorsement of the truth that God actively "works for the good of those who love Him, who have been called according to His purpose."[17]

This doctrine of providence is not an easy truth to accept, but once we do accept it, our appreciation of God's ways is deepened. "God has not been trying an experiment on my faith or love in order to find out their quality", wrote C. S. Lewis. "He knew it already. It was I who didn't. In this trial He makes us occupy the dock, the witness box, and the bench all at once. He always knew that my temple was a house of cards. His only way of making me realize the fact was to knock it down."

Grieving is a process and may be complicated by emotions such as guilt, anger and fear. Even when we seem to have dealt with each of these in turn, the process has not ended. Months, even a year or two, may elapse before life becomes relatively stable. We need to recognize that there are people who never face reality. To the end of their days they continue to grieve, a burden to themselves and to others.

16. 1 John 4:18   17. Romans 8:28

The Relief of Grief

"I tell you the truth, whatever you did for one of the least of these brothers of mine, you did for me."
(Matthew 25:40)

All probably agree that help is needed for the grief-stricken, but who is to do what? Or perhaps we ought to make the query more personal, "What can *I* do?" — a question often asked in the hope that nothing will be necessary!

So often we exclude professional people from our thought at a time of death, whereas they may play a vital role. I thank God for the medical men whom we were privileged to have and for the nursing staff who attended my wife.

Dr. Beverley Raphael, former research psychiatrist at the University of Sydney, points out that the doctor as a helpful and objective outsider is one of the people most suited to assist the bereaved.

Occasionally a doctor will not agree that his role includes the family. This is particularly true when he does not himself have a secure philosophy of dying and death. Whatever the reason, his view must be respected.

When a doctor genuinely believes that the facts ought to be kept from a patient, he should be definite with the family and leave the decision in their hands. No matter how confident his prognosis, God is often pleased to grant recovery to a person who seems certain to die, or to take one who seems likely to recover. The experienced doctor is well aware of this, even though he may not ascribe such results to God.

What is gained by not telling the truth? Most patients know. Relatives show it in their faces; nurses take longer to answer the bell; doctors tend to hurry past the foot of the bed or put on a false cheerfulness. The patient senses that he is regarded as already dead just when he so desperately needs human contact.

A conspiracy of silence frustrates every relationship with the patient and may aggravate the grief of those who are bereaved. Instead of looking back to a relationship that was frank and perhaps mutually encouraging, their last memories are marred by recollections of deceit.

In particular, deceit jeopardizes pastoral care by the Christian minister. More than the patient's temporal welfare is at stake: he stands on the brink of eternity.

The 1662 Book of Common Prayer faces facts. In the Order for the Visitation of the Sick, the minister is to "examine him whether he repent him truly of his sins, and be in charity with all the world. . . let him then be admonished to make his will. . ."

Jay Adams advises ministers to warn their congregations well in advance that they intend to tell dying patients the truth. "The warrant to do so", he says, "in spite of family or physician, comes from God. The pastoral relationship demands a truthful ministry of the Word. . . It is important to speak of preparation for the possibility of death, for no one knows when another will die."

The Bible, the ideal manual for such a time, urges us to "put off falsehood and speak truthfully".[18] Why should we seek to disobey it? At a later date, most families are grateful when they recall the openness that followed "the moment of

18. Ephesians 4:25

truth". They are often comforted by the way the patient faced the end once he knew that it was inevitable.

Of course, each one of us knows (and generally dreads) the thought that one day it is almost certain that help will be needed by someone who is bereaved and there will be no one to whom we can "pass the buck".

Those who have experienced the death of one near to them, and who through their own grief have proved the reality of Christ and His promises, are naturally better prepared. But this ought not to deter those who have not encountered death. There must surely be a first time for us all.

Young people are no longer in the position to shrug off such a reminder. Many of their peers die, particularly as the road toll mounts. Someone who knew a dead person well can be a real comfort to the family.

Our main fear is inability to say or do the "right thing". Provided we are natural, there is no need to have a rehearsed role to play. A firm grip from a friend's hand, an arm on the shoulder or a kiss may speak louder than words. Tears, provided they are sincere and kept in reasonable check, are not out of place, even amongst what we might regard as "Anglo-Saxon reserve".

When it is convenient, a short prayer is generally helpful, or the assurance that you and others are upholding the family in prayer. You may simply wish to say, "I'm sorry", or that you also feel the loss.

There is no need for elaborate or prolonged sentences. The bereaved person is not capable of taking in much, so the main thing is to be sincere and to be brief.

Whatever you do say or do, never say, "If there is anything I can do, let me know". Either do what you can see needs doing, or avoid the subject of help altogether. One way for women to help is by providing a plate of cakes or a meal which can be frozen for later use. It's surprising how helpful such a gesture is at a time when cooking may be out of the question and visitors are calling at intervals for several days at least.

A letter is a permanent way of expressing one's feelings. Some of the most welcome that I received were those recalling some incident in the past or some aspect of my wife's personality which the writer found appealing. Whether conversing or writing, don't seek to avoid the subject of death. Use the word itself if need be. In whatever way you express sympathy, remember two points: *Be honest; be natural.*

Remember that friendship is not only needed at the time of death. The weeks and months ahead can be times of great loneliness, mostly because friends feel embarrassed or helpless and fail to keep in touch.

Hospitality, visiting, taking the bereaved to a social function, offering to care for the children for a while, mundane though they may seem, are gestures which will help bring stability to the emotionally disturbed.

Hope in our Grief

"Praise be to the God and Father of our Lord Jesus Christ, the Father of compassion and the God of all comfort, who comforts us in all our troubles, so that we can comfort those in any trouble with the comfort we ourselves have received from God."

(2 Corinthians 1:3,4)

Paul certainly knew how to write a letter of comfort (he also had the capacity to cut his readers to the quick!). The interesting thing is that when comfort was given to him, it was by a human agent, Titus.[19] He used this example to encourage the congregation at Corinth.

How ready is your local congregation to bring comfort in time of death? Will the burden be shared, or left to the minister? Is your church like the one which Paul mentioned, when he said that "if one part suffers, every part suffers with it"?[20]

Do you ever talk over with other members how best to help in time of serious trouble or death? Is a warm and genuine love a characteristic of each member, and does this love express itself in a practical way when needed? *No one ought ever to feel alone when a member of a church.*

Our own attitude to the bereaved will depend to a great extent upon our understanding of what the Bible has to say on death and resurrection.

19. 2 Corinthians 7:6f   20. 1 Corinthians 12:26

It reminds us that "If the earthly tent we live in (i.e., our body) is destroyed, we have a building from God, an eternal house in heaven, not built by human hands."[21]

No wonder the Bible talks of our "glorious hope"! Other faiths believe in the immortality of the soul; our distinctive belief is the resurrection of the body.

Christ's resurrection guarantees that those who die believing in Him shall one day be raised in His likeness to be with Him for ever.[22] Through Him, death has lost its victory.[23] We face death in the knowledge that he has delivered us from the fear of death and the coming wrath.[24]

It was this sort of assurance that justified Charles Wesley in his assertion, "They may say what they will about Methodism, but our people die well."

Loving concern and practical sympathy are necessary, but in the end they are stop-gap methods of help if not linked to the Christian certainty based on Christ alone. Like Him, we must be able to sympathise with others in their weakness. By prayer, wise use of the Scriptures, and possibly our own testimony, we ought to help the bereaved bear their grief.

Prayer enables us to share with a loving heavenly Father, to bring our requests to Him in the certain knowledge that as we ask according to His will, He hears us and is pleased to answer.[25]

The Bible was written to encourage us,[26] and as it builds us up, so we in turn ought to use that encouragement to help others.

I shall always remember the help of a Christian brother a few days after my wife's death. His first wife had died about 20 years before when he was 50. He sat with me in his home and

21. 2 Corinthians 5:1   22. 1 John 3:2
23. 1 Corinthians 15:55
24. Hebrews 2:15; 1 Thessalonians 1:10
25. 1 John 5:14f   26. Romans 15:4

asked me to tell him and his wife all about the previous few weeks. He knew from his own life the advice that was needed. He warned me that the greatest temptation would be self-pity; told me of the pitfalls to be expected; encouraged me to talk of our relationship. He knew how essential it is to *let the bereaved speak*.

There is frequently a need to review and talk over aspects of what is now irrevocably past. Such a review of the lost relationship is a vital psychological aspect of the mourning process; it is only when the process progresses satisfactorily that the loss is ultimately resolved.

Statements such as "You must often think of the time when you did such and such together", or "You must especially miss your husband when you remember that particular occasion", are ways of initiating discussion. Let there be honesty on the part of both parties.

A typical illustration of this is of a widow whose friends are talking with her when one remembers a humorous story about the husband. He stops himself telling it out of consideration for her and, like everyone else, steers the conversation away from her husband's life altogether.

Had he told the story, she probably would have laughed; perhaps there might have been a tear or two in her eyes, but she would have thought it wonderful that he was still remembered.

Part of the congregation's task as time goes by is to help keep the memory of loved ones alive, to show concern for one another, particularly when someone has suffered a loss and there is no close member of the family to sustain the bereaved member.

Absolute despair can bear down upon the bereaved if those about them will not let them talk of their memories. A feeling of utter worthlessness and despair, together with guilt and sleeplessness, may follow.

Through my own experience, I have learned how shallow much of my pastoral care for the bereaved had once been. Recently I had to visit a family where the only son had been killed in an accident. His photograph was on the sideboard. Once I might have ignored it or merely referred to it, but now I picked it up, commented upon the likeness, told how I remembered him and how he would be missed. This enabled the parents to express feelings which might otherwise have remained bottled up, and allowed our conversation to be more natural and helpful.

A major problem is that we are too fearful of showing emotion: "boys don't cry". Why shouldn't they? When Jesus wept at the grave of His friend Lazarus,[27] more than mere emotion was being expressed, but He *did* weep.

God gave us our emotions and we are foolish to ignore them. Rather than tears indicating a so-called nervous breakdown, they are often a safety valve to reduce the pressure that might otherwise cause a collapse.

The widow who does not weep for the "sake of the children" makes them doubt her love for their father and also intensifies, rather than relieves, the strain which is so very real for her.

The angry feelings of protest, the yearning, the sadness, the guilt, the anxieties and fears, all need to be acknowledged by the grieving person and to be expressed. This may be difficult for people who do not normally express their feelings, but it needs to be done.

Sedatives, tranquillizers and antidepressants may interfere with the process and may additionally set the pattern for a future lifetime of drug taking in response to stress. (Obviously the doctor's own attitude to death and bereavement will influence his medication. When he has not resolved his own attitude to death, he will hardly be in a

27. John 11:35

position to encourage others to recognize and express their own feelings).

Whatever is done at the time of bereavement, much needs to be done later, both on an individual and family basis. The same principles apply for the family as for the individual: open expression of the complex emotions of grief — the sadness, the anger, the guilt — needs to be encouraged. Memories should be shared, thoughts and feelings about the person who has gone ought to be the subject of conversation.

In the case of children, the bereavement response will be modified by age, the stage of personality development, and understanding of what death means.

Older children may grieve as much as adults do and require similar forms of assistance. Younger children, however, mostly show a modified response and often very little overt grief, perhaps showing instead the symptoms of withdrawal, naughtiness or regression to more infantile behaviour.

Nevertheless, their grief is substantial. They may need gentle encouragement to share feelings about what has happened, with perhaps parents and other family members, and the doctor himself.

New lives must be built, new relationships made both for young and old. The early negative period of falling down, tearing up and uprooting must be turned to positive ends. Changes ought not to be hasty; major decisions should be avoided for some time wherever possible. Early remarriage, the sale of the home, a change in employment, are some of the areas where caution is needed.

Our Blessed Hope

"Looking for the blessed hope and the appearing of the glory of our great God and Saviour, Christ Jesus."
(Titus 2:13)

Why is the Christian hope more than wishful thinking? It is a reality because Christ is our hope. Eternal life is our present possession and when we have this quality of life we know that we "shall never perish".[28]

Such reality enables us to be positive in our approach to the bereaved. When this reality is accompanied by some understanding of general counselling principles and procedures, our support is likely to be even more valuable.

Throughout the experience, whether we are grieving or seeking to comfort, remember that grief is real both for believer and unbeliever. There is one major difference: the believer does not grieve as those without hope.[29]

There is sorrow, not lasting despair; there is emotion, not forced stoicism; in the midst of intense loneliness, there is the reality of Christ's presence.

Time and again there will be verses from the Bible which speak to our needs. Many of them were written in the fire of affliction by men with heavy hearts who themselves have proved God to be all that He claims to be.

Those who have died in Christ have gone to be with Him,

28. John 3:36; 5:25; 10:28   29. 1 Thessalonians 4:13

which is far better.[30] One day our fellowship shall be restored at the climactic moment of all history when our Lord Jesus Christ returns in glory.

Many questions puzzle us; some of the answers elude us. This has ever been so. Those in the early church at Thessalonica were even more perplexed. To help them, Paul wrote two letters which are in the Bible.

In the first letter he offered his readers encouragement regarding those "asleep" (i.e., dead), and our ultimate relationship with them.

"We do not wish you to be ignorant, brethren, concerning those who are sleeping, lest you go on sorrowing like those who do not have hope.

"For if we believe that Jesus died and rose up, so also those who have fallen asleep, God will (through Jesus) bring with Him.

"For this we say to you by the word of the Lord, that we who are living, who are left until the coming of the Lord, will by no means precede those who have fallen asleep.

"For the Lord Himself, with a shout of command, with the voice of the archangel, and with the trumpet of God, shall descend from heaven!

"And the dead in Christ shall rise first; then we who are alive, who are left, shall be snatched up together with them in the clouds to meet the Lord in the air.

"Thus we shall be for ever with the Lord!

"Therefore comfort one another with these words."

1 Thessalonians 4:13-18

30. Philippians 1:23

ACKNOWLEDGEMENT

Grateful acknowledgement is made to the following sources:

Jay E. Adams, Shepherding God's Flock, Vol. 1 (Presbyterian and Reformed Publishing Co., Nutley, New Jersey, 1975).

Gladys M. Hunt, Don't Be Afraid To Die (Zondervan Publishing House, Grand Rapids, Michigan, 1975).

C. S. Lewis, A Grief Observed (Faber and Faber, London, 1961).

Dr. Beverley Raphael, A Paradigm for Preventive Medicine; Coping With Grief (The Australian Church Record, September 7, 1972).

Dr. Granger E. Westberg, Good Grief (Augustana Press, Rock Island, Illinois, 1962).